PR
HOME   Y

A Guide to Safer Urban Living

by Alex Haddox

2/21/12

To Jason,

Wishing you and your family
health and safety.

Alex Haddox

PALLADIUM
EDUCATION, INC.

Published by
Palladium Education, Inc.
50 S. Delacey Avenue, Suite 202
Pasadena, CA 91105
http://www.palladium-education.com

Cover design and layout by Nicki Hovanec.

Tae Kwon Do Times magazine may have published selections of this book.
http://www.taekwondotimes.com

ISBN-13: 978-0615551920 (Palladium Education, Inc.)
ISBN-10: 0615551920

NOTICE OF LIABILITY

ACKNOWLEDGEMENTS

No one can realistically claim to be a security expert under self-tutelage alone. Everyone has had at least one guide, mentor, teacher or role model. I have had the honor of studying under multiple world-class martial art masters and experts in the self-protection field. I would not be in the position I am today without their skilled and knowledgeable guidance.

This work is a reflection of their teachings merged with my own experiences, interpretations, research and updates. Of these great men and women the most influential and consistent of my instructors have been my father Victor Haddox, father figure Bill Green, and Jim Wagner. I cannot thank them enough for their expert guidance and life-saving advice.

From the thousands of listeners of my weekly podcast, Practical Defense, I receive daily emails with commentary, suggestions, stories, questions, expert tips, and new interpretations of security protocols. You have influenced and pushed me to constantly reevaluate protocols based upon your real-world experiences and scenarios. I have learned as much from you as you have learned from me.

Finally, these books would never have come to pass without the support and editing skills of my wife Stefani, son Skyler and mentor Bill Green. They gave up their time so that I could spend it with you, the reader.

CONTENTS

PREFACE

I have been a victim of crime. Family and close friends have been the victims of crime, sometimes even violent crime. I begin this volume by sharing a few of my personal experiences with criminals from the perspective of the victim and from one who had a view into criminal dealings. I will share stories in specific sections of the book as real-world examples. These experiences are the inspiration for my lifelong professional interest in self-protection. I learned from my experiences, my observations and from many wonderful instructors. These volumes are a culmination of decades of experience I am sharing as a "Guide to Safer Urban Living."

While it is difficult to pinpoint my awakening to the threat posed by criminals, my memories from around the age of four are strongest. When I was little, my father worked in the federal prison system as a psychiatrist specializing in the treatment of the sociopathic criminally insane. He spent his days treating irrevocably broken men and women. These prisoners demonstrated no hesitation in taking the life of another. They had no love, no compassion, no caring, and no empathy dangerously coupled with a complete lack of impulse control. The feelings of others were meaningless. If you had something they wanted they would kill to have it without a moment's hesitation or remorse. You could share a pleasant conversation with one of these convicts and he would slit your throat without breaking the smile upon his face.

Some nights while my father was on duty at the prison my mother would receive threatening phone calls to our home. The caller would say her full name, the name of my father, describe what my father was wearing that night, our home address and then promise to visit our home to kill us all. Unsurprisingly, this would unsettle my mother so much she would gather my younger sisters and me into the master bedroom and hole up until my father arrived from work hours later. The callers were always inmates of the prison where my father worked and often his patients.

At the age of four I did not completely understand what was happening, but I did comprehend that there were bad guys out there who were threatening to hurt us and that we needed to be watchful. They called our house, so they knew where we were, and they had really scared my mother. It was not much, but it was enough to understand the threat of truly bad people.

My family's exposure to such an extreme criminal element resulted in strict home security protocols. We were constantly drilled and posed with "what if" scenarios and the appropriate responses. For example, I was not allowed to answer the phone until I was a nearly a teenager, we were never allowed to answer the door and we used passwords and codes in the event an approved family friend ever had to pick us up from school. We implemented these techniques decades before they entered common knowledge. My sisters and I still teach these techniques to our own children, and I teach them as part of my self-protection courses. They will be found later in this volume.

Later experiences only solidified my awareness of the threat posed by truly dangerous, aberrant individuals. Before I turned six I was approached on the street by two men offering me candy to get into their truck with them. This was within a block of my home while I was out playing in the neighborhood. I can still picture the yellow pickup truck with a white camper shell and the short, curly blond hair of the man in the passenger seat who made the offer. I said, "No," stayed out of reach, and went immediately home (I was well-trained by my parents). My mother called the police and two very intimidating officers in dark uniforms interviewed me in our living room.

A few years later, in a different home and neighborhood, our next-door neighbor was murdered in his home. I do not recall the exact details, but drugs were allegedly involved. A year later, a neighbor on the hill behind our home was the victim of home invasion, robbery and sexual assault. Men broke into her house while she and her son were home. They tied them both up and raped the mother repeatedly over the course of four hours. After they finally left with her valuables, she escaped her bonds and ran to a neighbor's home.

At ten my family experienced a tremendous blow, emotionally and economically at the hands of criminals. Our home was burglarized and burned to the ground while we were away for a single weekend. We returned to a smoking ruin.

The incident began a few weeks before. My father was mugged in his office parking lot in Downtown Los Angeles after work. He was loading books into the trunk of his car when someone snuck behind him and knocked him out cold. He stole his wallet. Another parking lot patron found him sometime later still unconscious, dangling from the trunk of his car.

My father's wallet was a goldmine to the professional criminal. In a horrible twist of fate, my father had arranged to buy a piece of jewelry for my mother from an acquaintance that night. As a result, he had an unusually large sum of cash in his wallet when he was mugged. Also in his wallet was a receipt for a condominium rental in two weeks. This thug had hit the motherload. He had my father's name, our home address, a large sum of cash and dates when we were going to be out of town.

Based upon how the burglary was conducted we can conclude the criminal was a professional and planned the event. He drugged our two large dogs who were in the backyard, he hired a moving van and emptied the home of even the furniture. He tore out walls looking for hidden safes (which we had). Additionally he stole my mother's Mercedes and in a final move, he set fire to our home destroying any evidence that might have been left behind. The furniture and safes should have remained in some form after the fire, but none could be found.

Due to the risk posed by brush fires every year, insurance companies would not issue fire coverage to homes in our neighborhood. We lost everything except for a few items in the garage and the clothes we brought for our weekend vacation. Consequently, there was no insurance money to rebuild or recover lost items. As promised years before, the bad guys had come to our home and destroyed our lives. It was the first time I saw my father cry. We spent months living with relatives.

Later in high school I found myself surrounded by crime. I was aware of teenagers who, instead of getting jobs to earn money, would rather steal car stereos, scooters, motorcycles and even entire cars. They would sell the hot vehicles to chop shops for quick cash. I knew one guy who when "knocking" cars in the wrong area was caught by a rival group. Years later he still bore the mark of the beating he took, including a permanent imprint of a baseball bat in his ribcage.

Some in this group were also on the forefront of identity theft. They would obtain blank birth certificates and create an entire identity. One member of the group would put on a disguise and use the birth certificate to obtain a state-issued driver's license and Social Security card. He or she would then open a bank account with real cash. The checks were mailed to a random address of someone whom they checked the mailbox. The group would go on a check-writing spree lasting a few days, using the completely valid driver's license and bank-issued checks; they would buy tens of thousands of dollars worth of clothes and other items. After the spree, they would discard the identity and never use it again.

Still other were interstate drug traffickers. For $3,000 cash, they would drive a stolen car packed with drugs from Southern California to other states. When the car was dropped off, they were provided with a plane ticket home. To a teenager, $3,000 in a single weekend was a lot of money so they made frequent runs.

Hopefully most of these people matured and stopped committing crimes. I suspect those that did not were eventually caught and went to jail or prison.

Sadly I have relatives who committed crimes as well. Their behaviors were driven by drug and alcohol abuse. My paternal grandfather would get drunk and head to the long-haul truck stops to fight. He was a powerful and arrogant man who felt the need to prove his prowess. At the time, the long-haul truckers had the reputation as being the toughest breed. Sometimes he won, sometimes he lost and he almost always landed in jail. My great aunts would throw him a party every time he was released from jail, much to the anger of my grandmother.

I also have relatives who were convicted of burglary and armed robbery. In all of these cases they were obtaining money to feed their drug addictions. All served time in jail and a few served years in prison.

Using my experiences, insight and research, I hope to help others protect themselves against the criminal element. I do not pretend to have experienced or know everything, but what insight I do have I willingly share.

Credentials

Below is a brief list of my credentials and formal education:

Black Belt, American Kenpo
Sr. Master of the Art Mohamad Tabatabai

Brown-Stripe, Hapkido
Grand Master Bong Soo Han

Certified Instructor, Kubotan Self-Defense
Soke Takayuki Kubota

Certified Firearms Instructor:

National Rifle Association
- Pistol
- Shotgun
- Rifle
- Personal Protection In The Home
- Personal Protection Outside The Home

Level 3 Instructor, Jim Wagner's Reality-Based Personal Protection System Jim Wagner

Certified Security Professional with firearm and pepper spray
California Bureau of Security and Investigative Services

Instructor, "Workplace Violence: Understanding and Prevention"

B.S., Business Administration

M.A., Adult Education and Training

INTRODUCTION

The purpose of this work and others in the series is not to turn readers into a bunch of scared rabbits sprinting frantically back and forth between secured locations. Crime is an unfortunate reality in our increasingly compacted urban communities. I hope to provide educational insight that equips people to better protect themselves. Blind or misguided fear is as dangerous and debilitating as complete ignorance. As a self-protection practitioner and instructor I walk a fine line between education and fear mongering. I hope readers gain insight into how crimes happen and learn techniques that can be incorporated into personal lifestyles that will better protect them and their loved ones from harm.

Before diving into the core material, there are a few guiding principles that everyone interested in self-protection must understand. These principles apply equally in all areas of personal security.

You Are Not the Police

Most people want to be heroes. Many train, practice, run "what if" scenarios and obtain concealed weapons permits with the secret hope of one day saving another person's life and catching the bad guy. This is a dangerous dream. As a citizen, your only goal is to protect yourself and those under your immediate care followed rapidly by escape. You are not part of security or law enforcement. You are not expected or required to attempt to contain or capture a criminal, even if he is in your home.

Unless you are sworn law enforcement or on-duty as a professional security officer, after defending yourself, let the criminal run away. Engaging a drug-addled, sociopath, or potentially mentally unbalanced criminal is a risk not worth taking. Let the bad guy run away and leave the chase to the professionals.

With this recommendation, a common response is that by letting the bad guy go, we are letting him escape to hurt others or that we are reinforcing his bad behavior. First, it is impossible to account for every scenario; this is a general recommendation that may not fit every possible permutation in life's infinite possibilities. Second, the time for parenting is long gone. Any action taken is not going to change his behavior. Most likely he will alter his actions to be more careful in victim selection, but resistance will not end his persistent bad behavior. It will end that incident which is desirable, however what drove him to commit the crime will remain regardless of what we do. Third, I am not suggesting that you simply give in to the criminal. If you have successfully defended yourself from attack, it is acceptable to let him go. You have that option. If you opt to forgo that choice, be aware that attempting to contain a violent criminal adds an additional level of complexity, physical risk and legal liability that few pause to consider. Sworn law enforcement officers have legal protections and levels of training far greater than the average citizen. Consider the risk versus reward. Is your life or physical well-being worth capturing this violent criminal? Is potential permanent debilitating harm to you worth the end result to your family? Also consider personal liability issues. Criminals have successfully sued victims for causing them permanent disability.

Next, also consider that there may be other bad guys lurking about. If I am with my family, I will not leave them defenseless while I chase down a single bad guy. Criminals often work in teams, even if you do not initially recognize them for what they truly are. The risk of leaving my family vulnerable to attack is too great.

You are not the police. Let the bad guy go.

Be the First to Call 911

Criminals know the legal system better than most of the population and they will use that knowledge against you. One trick used by criminals is to accuse the victim of attacking or assaulting them. That turns the incident into a "he-said, she-said" headache for the responding officer and court system to figure out. Sometimes the victim can be clearly identified. However in many instances, especially those taking place in public areas, the real victim can be unclear to the responding officer. The trick is, right or wrong, the first person to call into 911 is given more weight to the claim of being a victim. The theory is victims report crimes, not criminals.

CASE STUDY

Here is a hypothetical event with realistic responses. A man is walking down the street minding his own business. A bad guy jumps out from behind a building, brandishes a knife and demands the man's wallet, watch and keys to his car. In this case the criminal has exercised poor victim selection, because this citizen is legally armed with a handgun. The citizen draws his handgun, points it at the criminal and orders him to get down on the ground. Instead of complying, the criminal runs away. The citizen elects not to chase the bad guy down, holsters his handgun and enters the nearest cafe to have a drink to steady his nerves.

Thus far in this scenario, an armed citizen successfully and legally defended himself against and armed assailant. However, this event is far from over.

The criminal is angry. He does not like the citizen was armed and he did not get the money needed to buy his next drug fix. In order to retaliate against the citizen, he calls 911 from the nearest public phone and reports the citizen as attacking him. He gives a description of the citizen, what he was wearing, his height, his weight, age, where he saw him last and repeatedly states that he pointed a gun at him for no reason. The criminal hangs up the phone and disappears never to be heard from again. The police now have a description of the legally armed citizen, a report that he is threatening random people on the street with a handgun and his location. In the eyes of the responding police, he is a dangerous criminal and a threat to everyone in his vicinity. The police dispatcher sends squad cars towards the citizen, warning them the citizen is armed and dangerous.

At the same time, a witness across the street (thinks) she saw everything. She saw two men exchange words and then Man A (our armed citizen) pulled a gun on Man B (the criminal), and then Man B ran away. She never saw the knife, she saw only the hand-cannon wielded by our armed citizen. She also calls 911 and provides a nearly identical description of our armed citizen as the aggressor and course of events similar to those reported by the criminal. Our armed citizen now has two reports against him as being a gun-wielding maniac and threat to society. The police dispatcher sends more cars to the scene hunting for our citizen.

Meanwhile, our honest citizen and victim of a knife-wielding criminal assault, is finishing his latte, calming down some and considering that perhaps he should report the incident to the police. Suddenly, ten squad cars roll up on him with sirens blaring. They identify him from two eyewitness descriptions and draw on him. Our honest citizen's day has gone from bad to worse. First he faced a criminal attempting to rob him at knife point to facing 14 officers pointing various firearms at him. Why? Because he did not immediately call 911, report the event and establish himself as the victim.

Be the first to call 911.

The same sort of scenario can be applied to a home invasion. The criminal enters the home by some means and is confronted by a defiant and armed citizen. The criminal runs away, calls the police and reports the homeowner as a crazed, gun-wielding maniac who threatened his life. He describes the homeowner, gives the address and disappears. Events follow in a similar pattern to the first example.

CASE STUDY

A teammate of mine spent 30-days in jail because he could not adequately prove his innocence after successfully defending himself against three would-be muggers.

Jonn was huge. He was simply massive and there was not an ounce of fat on him. Jonn was a few years older than me, so I was still in high school when he moved on to college. One day while he was waiting for the bus on a college campus, three guys approached him and tried to rob him. He defended himself against all three of his attackers and in the process picked up the bench he had been sitting on and hit them with it.

When the police got involved, the three would-be robbers accused Jonn of attacking them. Jonn claimed that they tried to rob him, but because of the way he explained himself and also probably because of his size the responding officer did not believe him. Jonn was cited, eventually convicted of assault and spent 30 days in jail for defending himself against would-be robbers.

Be the first to call 911.

Recognize that violent crimes last far longer than they do in the movies. In real life, people just do not exchange blows and walk away. The hero does not drive home from the scene of the crime wrapped in a blanket surrounded by his adoring family. Law enforcement gets involved, follow-ups are conducted and sometimes even court appearances are required. A single incident that lasted a mere ten-seconds could take months or years to resolve.

Prepare yourself for a better defense by being the first to call 911.

Things

No *thing* is worth a life: Your life or even the life of the criminal. Stuff can be replaced. Life cannot.

Do not risk your life to protect a thing. Even if it is an heirloom, it is not worth your life. Your grandmother would not want you to risk your life over her ring, a television set or game system. All material items can be replaced with time and money. Money is a renewable resource; you have one life that is not.

Consider: Would your parents, wife, brothers, sisters or children prefer to have you or that thing?

Do not sacrifice your life or limb for a mere object. That is a waste a perfectly serviceable person.

Patterns Kill

Humans are creatures of habit. We prefer the regularity of patterns. Keeping to a consistent schedule is comforting and allows us to perform our daily activities with little thought. Unfortunately, regularity has inherent risks.

Repeating your daily activities at the same time every day makes you predictable and being predictable makes you a soft target. Someone who means you harm can accurately predict your specific location at a particular time or where you will not be at a particular time. Consider deer hunters. Deer are creatures of habit. Hunters study their habits and place deer stands along their favorite trails. The deer then blithely walk into an ambush. Contrast that with a wild boar. Pigs are nomadic and rarely follow a set pattern. They are also ferocious and will fight even when mortally wounded. Deer are soft targets; boars are hard targets. Be a wild boar.

Anytime a person reports a stalker to the police, whether a celebrity or average citizen, the first law enforcement recommendation is to change his or her schedule. Break those habits and throw the person who is tracking you off the trail.

Shifting daily schedules is not easy. It takes conscious effort and diligence. Here are some things worth considering:

- Change the time you leave for work.
  Leave earlier than normal. Sometimes, arrive later.
- Change the time children are taken to school.
- Change the time and location you pick up the children up from school.

- Change the time you go to the dojo or gym.
- Change the route taken to work.
- Change the route home.
  If you run out for an errand, take alternate ways to the store and others home.
- Turn off the lights in your home early or even leave the odd light on all night long.
  Timers with a randomizer are good for this.

In most big cities, especially in the US, most streets are laid out on a grid. This makes it is easy to vary the pattern taken without actually changing the time it takes or the distance.

Realistically, there are some things that we cannot change, but alter what we can. Incorporating randomness into our lifestyles will help keep us safer. It makes for a more difficult target.

Awareness

Awareness is a key to a safe and worry free life. Awareness goes hand in hand with avoidance. The first step in being able to avoid a potentially dangerous situation is to first recognize that the potential situation exists. This entire book is dedicated to providing awareness and avoidance techniques to help keep our families and us safer.

A misconception of awareness is that it causes disquiet and paranoia. In reality, a moderate level of awareness reduces stress and anxiety. Being aware of our surroundings is restful because we are in tune with the environment and can rest easy that there are no threats. Recognizing that no threat exists and the knowledge that if something were to arise we will catch it early is comforting.

Five Levels of Awareness

There are five (5) levels of awareness and they are identified by color. The original civilian color-coding system was developed by Col. Jeff Cooper and is often called the "Cooper Color Code." The original system used by the military included five colors and the civilian version often only uses four colors. I follow my instructor and friend's direction, Massad Ayoob, and teach all five colors to my students.

Color Conditions

White
This is a complete lack of awareness. This individual is focused internally and is oblivious to potential problems in his or her immediate environment. This individual has let his or her guard completely down.

Yellow
This condition is relaxed awareness. This is the preferred condition when out in public and the workplace. This person is aware of potential threats, but as no threat is immediately visible, he or she remains relaxed.

Orange
A specific potential or realized danger has been identified. This is a condition of heightened awareness; we are on alert. Actions are taken to avoid a potential conflict. Children and other people under our protection are being shielded. Avoidance techniques are being employed.

Red
This is the conflict condition. The defender is actively engaged in self-protection. This includes physical defense, taking cover, escaping or any combination thereof.

Black
Condition black is when the body is so overloaded with stimuli that the brain shuts down. The defender is unable to comprehend or respond to the immediate threat.

We strive to avoid living in Condition White. We no longer have to be aware of our surroundings to protect against changes in the weather or four-legged predators so we have lost many of our awareness skills and the understanding of the threats in our environment. This lack of awareness puts us at risk. Our greatest threat today is from the occasional two-legged predator who looks, smells and acts just like us (until he strikes). Our urban societies have placed so many false protections around us that we have forgotten how to recognize real danger. When we are presented with a true threat, we often think to ourselves, "This can't be happening to me. I'm a good person and I'm in a nice neighborhood."

The goal should be to live in Condition Yellow, relaxed awareness. This is a happy zone where we keep a passive eye to potential threats. Many people misunderstand Condition Yellow to be a state of paranoia. Nothing could be further from the truth. In this state we can relax and enjoy our surroundings with the understanding that we will recognize true threats when they arise. When no threats are present, we can allocate more attention to other things that matter such as our family and children. Our enhanced awareness also allows us to fully enjoy our surroundings. We see more, hear more and smell more. We are more in tune with the environment us and thus share a deeper relationship with our surroundings.

Achieving a persistent Condition Yellow is not instinctual in today's urban environment. In the beginning it will take a conscious effort to stay in Condition Yellow. However, after a few weeks of diligent effort it will become an unconscious habit, part of the self-protection toolkit. Once ingrained into our person, we will not be aware of doing it until a threat appears and it is thrust to the forefront of conscious thought. Once we achieve a relaxed, yet aware, state we can remain stress-free with the knowledge we will be warned if a true danger presents itself. Until then, we can enjoy ourselves in quiet comfort.

I am often asked where people can learn relaxed awareness. One of the best sources is Theravada Buddhist meditation. The practice is called Insight Meditation, Vipassana Meditation, or Mindfulness Meditation. Courses and lectures are often free and available all over the country (and world). There are also free podcasts that offer Insight Meditation training and guided meditation sessions. My favorite is "Zencast" with Gil Fronsdal (www.zencast.org).

ABOUT THIS BOOK

The security tips presented here are not guaranteed to prevent a break-in to your home. No one can guarantee that. These are recommendations and suggestions that will help keep you safer and more secure. The unfortunate reality is that if someone really wants to hurt you or wants your stuff, he or she is going to figure out a way to get it. There are also circumstances where you have done everything perfectly, you have taken every precaution and you are the victim of a criminal agenda. Stuff happens.

Home security is similar to personal security. The goal is to become a hard target, make the home a place not worth the effort to steal from. Convince the criminal that the home is too much trouble to bother with and chances are he or she will move on to an easier "soft" target.

One challenge in determining whether or not you are successful is the absence of a burglary or home invasion. The only evidence that you avoided a potentially dangerous situation is the lack of a dangerous situation. Such statistics are near impossible to measure and quantify. For home security a zero is a good number to have.

The best home security includes multiple defense and aversion layers. This book divides your home environment into several sections and discusses multiple recommendations.

1. Fundamentals
Home security essentials that apply to the entire home environment
2. Exterior Perimeter
The area from the walls of the home out to the property line.
3. Interior Perimeter
The walls of the home including all doors and windows, regardless of the floor.
4. Interior Security Measures
Alarm systems, protocols and configurations.
5. Apartments
Multi-family living complexes.

Each section includes protocols, best practices, recommendations and processes to help keep your family safer.

3 FUNDAMENTALS

Arriving Home

Arriving home after a long day at work or from a night on the town to find your house has been broken into is one of the worst nightmares, but it happens. In addition to the damage repair and item replacement costs, there is an immense sense of violation. Breaking and entering is a common crime. It can be your car, your home, or even your business. So what do you do when arrive home and discover this event?

The first and most important thing is **do not enter the home**. There are many reasons for this precaution. The primary concern is that the criminals may still be inside. The most common reason for breaking and entering is to steal your valuables so they can be sold. Criminals can be desperate, agitated and not necessarily thinking clearly. You do not want to stumble into someone like that in an enclosed place.

Here are two examples of people coming across criminals in process of robbing them.

CASE STUDY

A friend of mine's mother came home from work for lunch, walked into her home, saw that it was trashed, grabbed the nearest wireless phone (not a mobile phone, but a cordless house phone), ran out to the front yard, and called the police from there. That is exactly the right thing to do.

When the police arrived they told her they believed she walked into the middle of the burglary. The reason they think this is that the stereo equipment was not completely unhooked and the back door was slammed open. She came in the front, they heard her, and they ran out the back (empty-handed) while she ran out the front to make the call.

CASE STUDY

Criminals broke into a school. The maintenance worker was the first to discover the thefts before the students started arriving and he called the school police. While he was on the phone he saw a couple of teenagers running out of the building carrying computer equipment. They left with a couple of computers and a digital camera.

One never knows what type of criminal you might come across, so it is safest to avoid them whenever possible. If you arrive home and find your house has been broken into, **do not enter**. Stay outside and call the police from a mobile phone, a cordless phone or a neighbor's phone from a safe distance. Let the trained professionals wearing body armor and wielding guns clear your home. Do not attempt to clear the home yourself.

No *thing* is worth a life: Your life or even the life of the criminal. Items can be replaced; a life cannot.

Telephones

Phones are a powerful defensive tool. A telephone can be a lifeline to requesting help. Cordless landline phones are wonderful, but generally require extra electricity to run the base station and electricity can go out by an act of nature or the hand of man. For safety, ensure you have a no-frills corded phone that will work even when the electricity goes out. Corded phones should be in the bedrooms and a designated safe room. Often criminals that plan a home invasion will cut the power to the home before entering in an attempt to disable lights, alarm systems and phones in the home. Another trick used by criminals is to take the first phone they come across off the hook to prevent outgoing calls.

One way to counter these tactics is to keep a cell/mobile phone at the bedside. Move the mobile phone charger to the bedside to charge it overnight.

Julie Greene, author of *DEFY the Bad Guy Powerful Practical Self-Defense Strategies for Every Woman*, recommends practicing dialing 911 (with the battery removed). Her research suggests that many calls to Emergency Services never complete because under stress, the caller fails to hit the "Send" button.

See *Phone Protocols* in a later chapter for a list of items to report to Emergency Services.

Telephones are not a perfect defense and supply no shield if a criminal is already in the home. Once the call is made, it may be necessary to provide security for one's self or family until help arrives. In some cases, this can be as long as fifteen (15) minutes. It is important to remember that the help response time starts the moment the call is made, not the moment the incident begins. The longer you wait to make the call, the longer you are at risk.

EXTERIOR PERIMETER

Lights

The first home security recommendation is lights. Effective lighting is easy, cheap and highly effective. Criminals do not like to be seen while they are doing their thing. Lights make them visible and that makes them feel uncomfortable. Every home security recommendation list, every police officer and every security expert places lighting at the top of their list. The home and all vulnerable areas around your property must have proper illumination. At a minimum all windows and doors should be lit. A better system includes all sides of the home. Therefore, the front, sides and back should all have lighting.

Why the back of the home? Even if the front and the sides of the home have proper coverage, it is easy for a burglar to creep down on your neighbor's property, who may not have taken the same precautions, and hop the wall into your darkened backyard. What is a wall or fence to a criminal? Nothing. It is merely a minor inconvenience or something to use to hide behind. This is the trap we as honest citizens fall into; we see a wall as a barrier, as a line that says, "Do not cross." A wall has no meaning to the criminal. The social norms that bind society together, the unwritten rules of community that make life possible in our compacted urban environments do not apply to the criminal. They have little regard for laws. In many cases they use them to gain an advantage over others when citizens confront them.

The rear of the home should be treated with as much attention as the front. As you lock your front door and light it up, you should also lock your back doors and light them up as well. Consider your backyard's environment at night. Is it walled in on three sides, does it have high bushes or shrubs to keep the neighbor's prying eyes away and dampen noise from the kids (yours and theirs), and it is dark? The backyard is often a perfect working environment for the burglar.

Light placement should be considered. Once the architecture is determined, then the appropriate purchases can be made and installed. At a minimum, lighting should cover the front door, side doors, back doors and any garage entrances. If there are other vulnerable areas, illuminate those as well. Walk around the home after dark and look at it with the eyes of a criminal. Where are the places to hide? How would a burglar move and stay hidden? Implement measures to help expose their movements. If you have children place a light outside their bedroom windows.

There are many types of lights and lighting possibilities. The good news is that all are effective so there are multiple options depending upon the type of property and budget. Every inch of the property need not be lit with blinding, high-intensity light. If some light is not going to deter the criminal, a whole lot of light might not do any better. There is a happy balance that is easy to achieve.

Of the lighting options available, the most common are the manual type that turn on with a switch. Think of a standard porch light attached to every home in America. Additionally, there are spotlights or flood lamps usually lit with halogen bulbs. These can also be activated manually with a switch.

The best are motion-sensitive lights. These stay off until something passes in front of a sensor that triggers the system and bathes the area in light. This saves on the power bill while still providing security. It also acts as a "gotcha" for anyone passing in front of it. It indicates,

"You have been caught creeping around." Motion-sensitive lights are probably a good choice for placing around bedroom windows. They are not always on, which is nice for people who might have trouble sleeping with constant light outside their window. However, when they trigger, the entire window frame glows providing a quiet alert.

The downside of motion-sensitive lights is that any number of things can trigger the light. I have had them trigger on neighborhood cats, skunks, raccoons and even a hammock left outside on a windy night. Product labels promise the lights will not trigger on something smaller than a dog, but they do. The lights will not trigger on something really small like mice, rats, squirrels or small birds, but anything cat-sized or larger will most likely cause the light to activate.

Neighbors should be considered when selecting the location to mount the lights. My sister had to relocate a motion-sensitive light installed on the side of her house. It kept triggering on critters crawling along the top of the fence separating her yard from her neighbors'. When it turned on, it sent blinding light directly into the neighbor's bedroom window waking them up. Thus among other items to bear in mind, also consider neighbor annoyance when selecting the location for lights.

There are lights that turn on and off either with a timer or built-in light sensor (called photoelectric or dusk-to-dawn lights). This way, once set, the only worry is changing burned out bulbs rather than remembering to turn them on before crawling into bed. I really like the light-sensing lights. They sense when it is getting dark and automatically turn on when the sun goes down and turn themselves off when the sun comes up. This is great for weather changes (like dark clouds) or seasonal changes when it gets darker earlier or later depending upon the time of year.

Once the location and type of lighting system has been selected, the next considerations are bulbs and brightness. As mentioned earlier, there is no need to go overboard on brightness. A fair amount of light to see by is all that is needed. Many security experts suggest lighting should illuminate 100-feet from the walls of the home. Of course, all suggestions must be taken in context. Consider your home's layout and any special circumstances. If you want something brighter, use something brighter. Always select what is most comfortable.

The new energy efficient compact florescent bulbs have many advantages over the filament bulbs. First, they provide a good amount of light while keeping the power bill under control. Second, they generate almost no heat. They are great for using in small, waterproof outdoor fixtures. Heat will cause premature bulb blowouts. They also have a much longer life than standard filament bulbs. The downside is that they are more expensive. However, the cost has dropped dramatically in the past few years and as the technology improves, the prices should continue to fall.

There are two choices for floodlights and spotlights. The first requires a fair amount of work. It calls for mounting and hard-wiring the lights to the side of the home and requires an electrician to connect the home's power. Generally, cutting holes in walls and siding are necessary. A super-handyman with experience in electrical work might be able to do it. If there any doubts, hire a professional. Hard-wired lights can also be linked so that when one triggers, all lights in the circuit are activated.

The second choice is to use solar-powered motion-sensitive spotlights. They have advantages over the hard-wired lights. First, these are easy to install; it takes about 15-minutes per light to install. Second, they work independently of the home's power. Power independence can come in handy if there is a power outage in your neighborhood, or if the burglar cuts the power to your home to circumvent any alarm system, the solar-powered lights will still be operational. Of course there are downsides as well. They are not nearly as bright as the hard-wired lights and the solar collector panel must be positioned so that it receives direct sunlight for a good portion of the day. If you live in a northern climate or snow or leaves collect on the panels it could be a problem.

Figure 1 - Sample Motion-Sensor Lighting (see page 24)

Cameras

Security cameras have come down significantly in price as technology has advanced reducing development, material and production costs. Cameras with features that were previously within the budget of banks and high security facilities are now affordable by the average homeowner. For a few hundred dollars the homeowner can include a camera with low-light sensors and motion detection based upon changes in the pixels of the image rather than heat.

If within the budget, cameras are an excellent layer to the overall home security system. A security camera visible from the street is a clear indication that the home is protected and by a serious system. Cameras are so common in a commercial environment they have lost their ability to deter criminals. However, due its rarity in the urban home environment, a security camera is an excellent visual deterrent to home invasion.

Security cameras are used to help catch the criminals after a home invasion or an attempted invasion. Other than the deterrent mentioned earlier, a camera can only bear mute witness to the events, documenting everything in its field of view. The recorded footage can also be used to prosecute the criminals once they are caught.

Finally, cameras can be used to view people at the door without placing you or your family at risk. If the viewing screen is portable (WiFi connected cameras and a tablet computer), you can even be in the backyard and see who is at the front door. Other options include connecting the camera to televisions and computers (laptop or desktop).

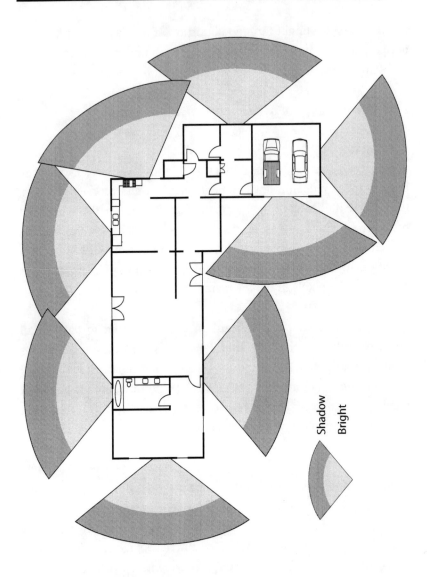

Figure 1 - Sample Motion-Sensor Lighting

Security cameras as part of an alarm system will be covered in detail later in this volume.

Gates and Walls

Gates, walls and fences prevent casual entrance to your property. The challenge is that most city home ordinances require that walls be no more than six-feet high although some allow as much as eight-feet in the backyard. These walls do more to protect privacy than keep criminals from accessing the property. Most young adults can hop a 6-foot wall without much effort. Law enforcement trains in specific techniques to scale 6-foot high walls without losing much momentum when chasing suspects. Therefore, perimeter walls should be considered privacy shields rather than true security devices.

Gates have challenges similar to perimeter walls with the added vulnerability of being weaker. The key point to gates is that they should be locked in addition to remaining shut. Although this does little in terms of a security measure, it can increase the legal defense should something happen. In the eyes of the court there is a difference between an unlocked gate (even if shut) and a locked gate. A locked gate helps strengthen the argument that entry to the property was unauthorized.

Shrubs and Plants

Thorny, prickly and generally unpleasant plants can be strategically placed about the home and property to deter criminals from attempting entry. Horticultural defenses can be used in ways otherwise prohibited by law with deterrents made by man. For example, local ordinances can limit the height of a wall, but there may be no restriction on the height of a tree with prickly leaves. Similarly, in nearly all circumstances, barbed or razor wire is strictly forbidden for use on urban home property, however, thorny or spiny bushes and flowers along the perimeter of the home and under a child's bedroom window are not.

Use landscaping to increase the security of the home. When selecting plants to place around the property, consider those with the dual-purpose of being visually pleasing with security. Strategically placed plants can add another level of security for the home.

As with all security measures, caution should be used when placing plants. Be certain not to place plants in locations that criminals can use to hide, scout, or use to access the property. Keep bushes below window level. In addition, it is illegal to use plants to block access to public areas. Do not use plants in areas that pose risk to the homeowners or guests. Similarly, do not select species that are dangerous to the homeowners or residents. For example, the Oleander bush is a dense shrub with stout limbs and beautiful flowers that thrives in a hot, dry climate. It is commonly found along the highways of the American South-West. However, parts of the Oleander are highly toxic. Ingesting a single leaf can kill a child, two leaves can kill an adult and 10-20 leaves can kill cows and horses.[2] Even inhaling the smoke from a fire made of Oleander wood is toxic. Oleander is a prime example of a plant that may make a good security barrier, but should be avoided around homes with children and pets.

Equipping Your Burglar

We all leave items strewn about our yards and patios. Take care not to leave items out that can be used to break into your home; avoid equipping a burglar. These are items such hammers, chisels, screwdrivers and ladders. If someone is going to attempt to break into your home, make him work for it. Do not provide the tools to use against you.

A challenge is that although your home may remain clear of items to be used against your home, your neighbor may not be as diligent. Unfortunately, it is easy for a criminal to hop into your neighbor's yard, grab a tool, and then use it against your home.

CASE STUDY

A good friend of mine witnessed a home burglary where the criminals used a ladder left out to enter a second story window. My friend was out on her back patio when she noticed a ladder go up against her neighbor's home. As she watched, two young men climbed the ladder and entered an open window on the second floor. She immediately called the police as she knew the elderly couple was not at home and the men entering were obviously not workmen.

The police arrived in time to catch the two burglars in the act and make an arrest. Unfortunately, the homeowners did not press charges and the two men were released. One of the men was a grandchild of the homeowners. She learned afterwards that he was looking to steal items and money to feed his drug habit. The grandparents could not bring themselves to put a family member in jail.

Misdirection

Items that can be used to break into your home should be stored out of sight in an inaccessible container. However, other items may be left out to misdirect a potential home invader and dissuade him from selecting your home.

Another good use of misdirection is to make it appear as if a large dog lives there. Leave large food and water bowls and chew toys in the yard within plain view of the street or someone poking his head over the wall. The appearance of a large dog can be a deterrent to someone sizing the property up for burglary. The food bowls and toys should look well used (chewed) and occasionally moved around. Just as with the boots, good sources for used dog toys are family, second-hand stores and neighborhood garage sales.

A passive measure that can be purchased for just a few dollars are security service stickers. These can be purchased from various places online and even eBay. Place these stickers on your windows and doors whether you have a security system installed or not. The idea is to look like you have a security system installed and thus convince a would-be burglar that you are not worth the effort.

Security and personal protection guru Massad Ayoob suggests considering displaying stickers for a security system other than the one installed. For example, if you have an ADT security system, use stickers for a Brinks system. In that way, if a thief tries to disable the electronic security, he will look for something different than what is installed. It is a method to confuse and make the crook feel uncomfortable, which is a highly desirable outcome.

CASE STUDY

A podcast listener from Australia made a fantastic suggestion for women living alone. A deterrent to a would-be home invader is to keep a big pair of men's shoes or boots out on the doorstep or front porch. The idea here is to make it appear that a big man lives at the home, rather than a single woman. Sources for well-used shoes or boots are a father, brothers, second-hand clothing stores or neighborhood garage sales.

Children's Toys

Keep children's toys out of sight from prying eyes. Unlike men's boots or dog toys, children's toys can entice criminals and pedophiles to break into the home. Toys in the yard distinguish your home as one with desirables inside. For the common burglar, toys in the yard suggest there may be other items of value in the home including gaming consoles, game DVDs and cartridges, computers and televisions. Small and portable electronics are high value items that can be sold quickly, thus making them a popular target for theft.

Holiday Trash

In the same way that toys in the yard suggest games and computer systems in the home, trash left out for pickup can also advertise valuables in the home. Packaging for high-value items should be cut up and placed into trash bins, rather than left intact and visible on the curb. Boxes for new laptops, desktop computers, televisions, monitors, DVD players, cameras and similar items not only alert the criminals to valuables in the home, they provide an exact inventory of recent purchases. Homes are most vulnerable around the winter holidays where gift exchanges hit a high for the year. Criminals have been known to patrol neighborhoods after major holidays looking at trash to select their targets.

Cut boxes into small pieces to make them fit into the bins. If the bin is filled and pieces remain, hold them until the next trash pickup cycle. It is better to wait a week than advertise your latest expensive gadget to every crook prowling the neighborhood.

CASE STUDY

One neighborhood rents a trailer or van after each major holiday. The community loads all flattened cartons for a trip to the local recycling facility. The money earned is used to pay for the rental.

5

INTERIOR PERIMETER SECURITY

Doors

Doors are the primary means of entering and leaving a home and that is where much of the focus is when someone wants to illegally enter. Doors are made to be opened, they are large enough to fit people and objects through and make little noise when used. The majority of home invasions and burglaries use a door to gain entrance.

All exterior doors should be solid-core without windows. A door should be a barrier to the environment and to anyone not invited into the home. A solid-core door will withstand kicking and battering more readily than a hollow-core door. A window allows two-way viewing into the home, which is not always desirable. Additionally, it is easy for a criminal to smash the window and reach in to unlock the door or disable door alarm sensors.

When someone knocks, one must be able to verify who that person is before the door is opened. Peepholes are the tools to be used to identify visitors. Installed at eye level, it enables the homeowner to see the other side.

Peepholes offer more protection than windows. For example, if there is some stranger outside the door, you should be able to see him without being seen. Windows provide two-way viewing whereas peepholes are one-direction. When selecting a peephole, be certain to get one that has a good field of view that will reveal someone trying to hide to the sides or below. Also, replace old peepholes. They are inexpensive (around $10 at your local hardware store) and take less than 2 minutes to install. Peepholes will become coated in grime, paint, hard water stains from sprinklers or rain and the older ones often do not have a great field of view.

Unfortunately, peepholes are not perfect. From the outside, especially if it is dark, it is possible to see inside light and movement (but no detail). Shadows cast from inside make it possible to determine when someone walks up to the door and bends over to squint through the little hole.

Next, install a quality deadbolt. Pin doorknob locks can be popped open easily and thus offer little security. A deadbolt will make it more difficult for someone to enter the home. With a good deadbolt the criminal has three choices: to try to pick it, crowbar the door, or kick it in. There are deadbolts models that have no key access from the outside. It is a deadbolt that does not show on the outside of the door; the entire mechanism is contained within the door. The single latch is on the inside so there is no way to pick it and it can only be locked and unlocked from the inside.

Change the locks when moving into a new property. One has no idea who has a key, especially if it is a rental property. If renting, offer to pay for the lock change. Often the owner will not let you change the locks yourself, so you might need to hire a professional locksmith. Fresh locks are worth the money and peace of mind.

These days thieves rarely pick locks. It takes skill and time, neither of which the average thug is going to have. Furthermore, thieves often do not care if the homeowner knows he or she has been robbed. The most common entry technique is the crowbar method. The thieves take a crowbar, jam it into the joint between the door and the doorframe where the locks are and pop the door by ripping the wooden doorframe apart. It takes less than 5 seconds. Crowbarring or kicking in a door to an empty home is often quiet enough for a quick snatch and grab.

CASE STUDY

I lived in apartment building where there were a series of crowbar break-ins. The thieves selected an apartment, checked to see that no one was home by knocking on the door repeatedly, placed masking tape over the peepholes of the surrounding apartments, crowbarred the door, placed valuables in a clothes basket, covered them with clothes and escaped. If passed in the hall, the thief looked like someone carrying a heavy basket of laundry to the community washers.

The apartments were repeatedly burglarized over the course of several months. Details were uncovered from the evidence left behind (such as the tape on the peepholes) and some video camera footage. Evidence suggests they knocked repeatedly on the doors because they did it to my sister *while she was home*. She was in the tub when there was a banging on the door. She ignored it for a while, not wanting to get out of the bath to answer the door. The knocking was so persistent that she finally got out to check the door and against better judgment, she opened the door. She was presented with four men. They claimed they were looking for the handyman and called him by name. She explained he was not working in her apartment and they thankfully moved on. 15 minutes later another apartment on a different floor was hit. The building handyman was not working that day.

The fact that they knew the building's layout and the handyman's name suggests that it was an inside job. The thieves were friends of a resident or they were former residents. The break-ins finally stopped after the building owner installed alarm systems in every apartment in the building and paid for 6-months of monitoring.

Interestingly, it was not the installation of the alarm systems that caused them to stop. After the installation of the alarms and stickers placed all over the site, there was one final break-in. The burglars used their normal process, popped the door open and triggered the alarm. In response to the alarm sounding, the invaders sheared the alarm control panel from the wall, which of course did nothing. They left the apartment empty handed. There were no further break-ins following that incident. A current resident would have known that the alarms were real and active while these criminals obviously did not take the stickers and signs seriously.

CASE STUDY

Another example of a violent or forceful entry into the home is from a string of neighborhood burglaries. A nice, quiet neighborhood located in a Los Angeles suburb where most of the residents were retirees who had lived there for several decades. These burglaries required a plan, a team of crooks and occurred during the day.

Evidence suggests (video footage and eyewitness accounts) it was at least a three-man team: the doorman or "lay off", a lookout, and a driver. The lookout is nearby in a car or on the sidewalk on talking on his or her cell phone. The driver is often down the block waiting for the signal to move in. The doorman is the person who approaches the front door.

The doorman walked up to the door and knocked or rang the bell. If no one answered, he kicked in the front door and looted the house. He would walk the house and gather all of the valuables by the front entryway. When he had everything, he called the driver using a cellular phone. The driver backed the car into the home's driveway. The two then loaded up the car and drove away. These crooks could empty a house of all valuables in less than 10 minutes. The lookout was picked up a few blocks away.

According to police reports, one poor victim was present when they attempted to enter her home. The elderly victim did not respond to the doorbell and knocking. Rather than answer the door, she watched the man through her peephole. She was incredibly surprised when he kicked in the door. As soon as the burglar realized there was someone home, he took off.

Police reports also indicated that when people did answer the door, the criminals gave some excuse for knocking such as, "Sorry, wrong house" or, "I'm looking for somebody."

One method to protect against a crowbar or kick-in method of entry is to install a steel doorframe. When a door is crowbared or kicked in, the doorframe often breaks first, not the door or locks. Former law enforcement SWAT team members insist that steel frame doors are not kicked in and that often hand-held battering rams do not work. Law Enforcement entry teams require special gear to penetrate reinforced doors with steel doorframes.

If replacing the entire doorframe is out of your budget, you can have a locksmith install wrap-around plates to reinforce a wood frame and wood door around the locks and hinges. This helps quite a bit, but still not as good as the steel framed door.

Alternatively, low-cost steel doorframe reinforcements are available for around $100.

CASE STUDY

A listener to the show self-installed steel doorframe reinforcements. He also reported that it prevented a break-in attempt into his home at 2:30 in the morning. Someone came to his door and spent several minutes attempting to kick in his door and was thwarted by the security device.

Lock Your Doors

Your front door may be as secure as a bank vault, but unless locked, it is worthless. There are many crimes of opportunity that happen when front doors to homes are left unlocked during the day.

Door-to-door salesmen or people hired to place advertisements, menus, coupons or business cards on doorsteps sometimes check the door to see if it is unlocked. If unlocked, they might step in to grab a few items left on the front table including wallets, purses, watches and keys. These people are not career burglars, but merely opportunistic thieves looking for a quick score.

Take a moment to consider how often you leave the house without locking the door. You are just going to be a few minutes and it is a great neighborhood, right? It might be a quick run to the store a block or two away, taking the dog around the block, or just a few seconds around the yard to pick up the paper or pull in the trash bins. Then a neighbor stops to chat and all of a sudden it has been 20 minutes and you are still across the street or a few houses down the road. These opportunist thieves have been known to grab items even while people are home, but in another part of house. They can be in and out in a few seconds while your back is turned.

In every neighborhood there are people canvassing the neighborhood leaving flyers, business cards, and menus on doors. Some hop security gates to leave items on porches. I find business cards for gardening, tree trimming, real estate, daycare, and menus on the doorstep daily.

Almost certainly the vast majority of these people are honest and hard working. However, hard times can make an honest person desperate. The temptation could be too much. Remove temptation and lock the door whenever you leave, for any reason, always!

CASE STUDY

In a Los Angeles neighborhood there were a series of opportunist thefts from homes. The robberies were eventually tracked to a group of a men hired from out of state to place marketing materials on doorsteps. There were about 25 people of which 5 had criminal| backgrounds. A police investigation and search uncovered that 3 had been stealing property from homes while they were placing the marketing materials. The company that hired the men had not performed background checks on the low-wage labor hired for the short duration contract. The suspects were arrested and all recovered property was returned to the homeowners.

CASE STUDY

A close friend experienced a home invasion and robbery. As many people in his neighborhood, he converted his non-attached garage to an office where he kept computer equipment. The garage was physically located in his backyard, behind a gate and out of view from the street. Because he felt secure, he rarely locked the door to his office.

One night, someone entered his backyard, walked into the office and removed computer equipment and remote controlled cars. They also tried the back door to his home and found it unlocked. The criminal then took advantage of the opportunity to enter the primary residence and remove wallets, purses and cellular phones from the kitchen.

The homeowner was awakened by a noise at around 2am and went to the kitchen. He found the back door open, closed it, locked it and returned to bed. The thefts were not discovered until nearly noon the following day. Even with the losses, the scariest aspect to the home invasion is the perps were within fifteen feet of two sleeping children, ages two and four-months at the time.

Keeping all perimeter doors locked extends to vehicles, even if they are parked in your home driveway. Criminals will not only check the doors to the home, they will check the doors of any car parked in the driveway. Items are often stolen from cars when doors are left unlocked.

CASE STUDY

A woman had her work laptop stolen out of the back of her car while it was parked in her home driveway. At the time she was not consistently locking her car door after she arrived home. Eventually someone happened upon her car while it was unlocked. The thief took his time and searched the car thoroughly. He uncovered a laptop buried in the storage compartment hidden under other items. It was not even stored in a laptop carrying case. The thief was forced to move things around and open several containers to find it.

This theft happened over the weekend and was not discovered until the back door swung open while she was driving Monday morning. Apparently the thief did not fully shut the door perhaps to avoid making any noise.

Pet Doors

Holes cut into doors to allow pets access to and from the home are a significant liability and should be avoided. The pet doors provide access not only for your pet, but other neighborhood pets, feral animals, wild animals and criminals.

CASE STUDY

I interviewed a family friend and neighbor for my podcast, *Practical Defense*, about her sexual assault at the hands of a man who entered her home via a pet door. She lived in a very nice neighborhood. Her large Doberman Pincher had just died and they had a large pet door cut into the kitchen door to allow the dog free access to the property when the family was away at work and school.

While her family was just waking up to start their day, at about six in the morning, a man entered their home. She was just out the shower and bent over blow-drying her hair in the bathroom. Her 8-year old son was asleep in the master bedroom next to where she was. Her teenage son was in his room down the hall with the television on while he was getting ready for school. Her husband was asleep in the youngest child's room at the end of the hall (he moved to that room to sleep when the 8-year old crawled into the master bed during the night).

The first time she noticed the man was when he grabbed her from behind. She was looking down and noticed the shoes of the man standing behind her did not belong to her husband. She screamed and struggled to free herself as the man tried to shut to the bathroom door. Most of the noise was masked by the noise of the hair dryer. Her 16-year old son was the first to respond to her cries. He came to investigate, saw his mother struggling with the man, ran back to his room to get his baseball bat and returned to help his mother. The man realized help was coming, released her and ran from the house. Her elder son and husband chased the man out of the house and into an alley where they lost him. The 8-year old boy, who was 5-feet from the man trying to rape his mother, did not wake up.

Windows

Windows allow two-way viewing from and into the home. Windows help make a house a home (this is a security challenge). No one wants to live in a lightless dungeon. The unfortunate reality is windows are weak points in the interior perimeter of the home because glass is inherently brittle, breaks easily, and allows criminals to see into the home. Windows are the second most common entry point into the home.

Coatings can be applied to glass windows to make them smash resistant. This process is called glazing or laminating. The process turns a standard brittle window into something closer to security glass that still breaks, but the adhesive and resins prevent the glass from falling. The lamination is available in sheets, but tricky to install. It is similar to after-market window tinting for cars. However, just like window tinting for cars, if it is not installed by a professional or is cheap, it can bubble over time, look ugly and hinder the clarity of the view.

Glazing and laminating are not easily applied. Research the best options for the local climate and consider hiring a professional installer. There are many types, brands, and colors many with UV filtering.

Windows and frames can be upgraded to provide better insulation and better security. If the opportunity to replace an old or rotted window presents itself, consider security features during the selection process. Security coatings applied at the factory are far better than after-market options.

Window Coverings

Ensure the entire window is completely covered when selecting window dressings for privacy and security. The covering should overlap on all edges by a fair margin to help prevent someone from peeking in around the edges. Additionally, select a material that is dense enough to prevent shadows revealing movement when backlit. Light will always show through, but it is best to prevent someone on the outside determining if a resident is walking around the room.

Consider turning the blades on horizontal blinds up so that the blades are high on the inside and slope down and away to the outside. Horizontal blinds rarely shut tightly enough to block all sight into the room. With the blades high on the inside, the angle of vision of anyone outside the home is forced up. The field of view is restricted to the tops of shelves or the ceiling. It is not a perfect solution, but it does make things more difficult for a criminal inspecting the home.

Window Locks

A good security protocol is to immediately lock every window as it is shut. A burglar or home invader will often check windows to see if they are locked if he finds the front door inaccessible.

CASE STUDY

Several years ago there was a serial rapist who preyed upon women that left windows open or unlocked at night. He hunted during the warm summer months, prowling the neighborhood searching for opportunities. When he found a home with an open ground-floor bedroom window he would climb in and rape the victim. The sexual assaults appeared to be random with the selection made only by the opportunity of an open or unlocked window.

Second story windows should also be shut and locked. Someone who is mildly athletic can find his or her way into a second story window given enough time and a few tools found around a typical yard. In a team effort, one man can boost another into an open second story window in a matter of seconds.

All windows, first and second story, should remain shut and locked at night and when no one is at home.

Screens

Screen doors and window screens are meant to keep bugs from coming into the home, not criminals. In the hot summer months people often like to leave their windows open during the night to let the cool breezes into their homes and they can turn off the air conditioning for a bit. When asked if these people were worried about criminals crawling into the bedrooms or even their children's bedrooms, the common response was, "Its OK, we have screens."

If bug screens kept out criminals, banks would use them instead of steel vaults.

Screens are not even a minor inconvenience to criminals wanting to enter a home. Home invasion and rapes are more common during the summer months because people leave windows open at night for the fresh air.

CASE STUDY

My aunt and uncle experienced this exact type of home invasion and robbery because they left their bedroom door open with only the screen shut. They had a sliding glass door leading to a patio off of their bedroom. Someone hopped their 6-foot concrete wall, walked into the bedroom while they slept and stole my uncle's wallet and everything else of value off of their dresser. My aunt and uncle never woke up. They only discovered the theft late the next morning.

Shut and lock all windows on the first and second floor at night. If it is warm, run your air-conditioning. Bug screens will not keep criminals out of your home. Similarly, shut and lock all windows on the first and second floor when you leave for the day.

Service Boxes

Lock your fuse/circuit breaker box and phone junction box. The fuse/circuit breaker box is inside in most newer homes, but in older homes it is often on the outside of the house. Access to that box should be restricted and protected with at least a padlock. The fuse box gives a potential burglar or predator an easy way to cut the power to your entire home, including any wireless phones and alarm systems on the property. Few people still use hard-wired landline phones these days. If the power is cut, how can you call for help?

Similarly, how can you call for help if the phone lines were cut? The vast majority of the time the phone junction box is on the outside of the home or building. Access to the phone junction box should be restricted and protected with at least a padlock.

No Advertising

If you are a woman, do not advertise that fact, especially if you live alone. Refrain from placing cutesy items in the yard or on windowsills. Select items to make the home look nice without broadcasting. The key is not to be overt in the décor.

Similarly, do not publish your name in common areas. Do not place signs proclaiming "The Johnson's" in the yard, driveway entrance, or mailboxes. If name are required on community mailboxes (for apartment complexes), just use a first initial and last name. One of the worst things a woman can do it put out something that says "Janine's Place."

Consider placing signs that misdirect strangers as to who you are and your family's makeup. I have heard from postal delivery employees that listen to my podcast explain they ignore names posted on the property. Mail and packages are delivered to the address, not the name.

Garages

An attached garage is an entry point into the home. Depending upon the when the home was built, there may be a door connecting the inside of the home to the garage. It is a mistake to consider and treat the door connecting the home to the garage as interior door rather than an exterior. For security purposes, treat the garage as outside the home rather than inside.

The garage is segmented from the home itself with fire-hardened materials. The walls that line the garage are not normal interior or exterior walls. They are filled with dense material. If a fire starts in the garage (where solvents are stored, cars are filled with gasoline, and other flammables are stored on shelves and in cabinets) it has less of a chance to spread to the rest of the house.

This dense material also has sound dampening properties. Therefore, if someone breaks the window in the garage, it might not be heard as easily as if someone broke the window in the living room.

Garage doors come with default opening codes. Few people take the time to change the code after a new unit is installed or even after the installer leaves. Fewer still change the codes after moving into a new property. This begs the question, "How many people can open our garage doors?"

CASE STUDY

A reporter bought the most common type of garage remote, left it on the default setting and drove around his neighborhood to see how many garage doors he could open. He opened enough to where it caused quite a scandal.

Treat the garage as exterior to the home. Keep the door joining the home to the garage locked with a quality deadbolt and change the codes on the garage door remote.

Interior Security Measures

Alarm Systems

Alarm systems can secure the interior perimeter of the home. There are any number of sensors and sensor arrays that can be installed from a number of different companies. There are the sound sensors that listen for breaking glass, door and window sensors, motion detectors, integrated smoke and gas detectors, and video cameras. The list is enormous and features can be installed in any number of combinations. There are also a number of trigger settings. For example, there is a "home stay" setting where only the perimeter is set. The family can move freely about the house, but as soon as someone opens a window or door, the alarm triggers immediately (no countdown). In another example, there is the full lockdown mode when the home is empty. Alarm sensors are a great way to check to see if any doors or windows are left open when retiring at night.

The latest alarm systems are wired to the Internet. Subscribers can log into a service provider's website over a secured connection and check the status of the home at any time. Many companies also offer free mobile phone and tablet applications to manage alarms and review the trigger history. Parents can even check to see if a child is home when he or she is supposed to be by looking at log files. If an alarm triggers, the system can call the subscriber's cell phone, send an email and send a SMS text message with the details or even include a video clip from one or all of the video cameras. Some systems have battery backups and use cellular networks to connect to the monitoring company. That way, if the power goes out or if the phones go down (or they are cut), they system remains active and can still monitor the sensors, send alerts and call out for help. Some systems require a professional installer while others can be self-installed. There is an alarm system available to meet the needs and budget of just about everyone.

The downside to home alarms is that the police no longer respond to them. Too many false alarms have cost police departments too much money over time, so they no longer respond even if the monitoring company makes the call. The only way to get immediate help is for the monitoring company to send one of their private patrols to the residence or for you to dial 911 from the premises and ask for police assistance.

Alarm systems are not a perfect defense. They act as a deterrent and can scare off an intruder if he breaches the perimeter and triggers the alarm. However, alarms cannot protect against the smash and grab. Surveillance videos are broadcast on the news and posted to YouTube. Criminals break windows or drive cars through walls, setting off alarms, the criminals grab what they can, and then run before any sort of response can show up. Flashmob robberies are gaining popularity and the judicial system has upgraded laws to deal with this new criminal activity.

CASE STUDY

A homeowner recently experienced a snatch and grab burglary. He had just bought a new video camera and tripod. He spent the evening playing with it and left it setup in his living room, visible through a window to the street. Someone walking by decided he wanted it, so he picked up a brick, hurled it through the window, setting off the alarm, the perp jumped in, took the new camera and ran away with it. It took less than 10 seconds and the alarm offered little protection. The homeowner was out a few hundred dollars for a new window and a few thousand for a new video camera and gear.

Figure 2 - Sample Sensor Layout (see page 50)

Peering Into the Home

The best practice is to avoid placing valuable items in front of windows and doors visible from the street. The list of valuables includes:

- Televisions
- Computers
- Stereo
- Wallets and purses
- Gaming consoles
- Cameras
- Keys
- Garage door openers

All of these items are vulnerable to smash and grab strikes whether an alarm system is present and noticeable or not. Items such as keys or garage door openers may not have immediate value, however, they may lead to other items such as the car, garage or back into the home itself at a later date.

Additionally, items of value seen from the street may pique the curiosity of criminals passing by. If an item of value is clearly visible from the street, there may be items of equal or higher value elsewhere in the home. Generating curiosity in a criminal is an invitation to a burglary.

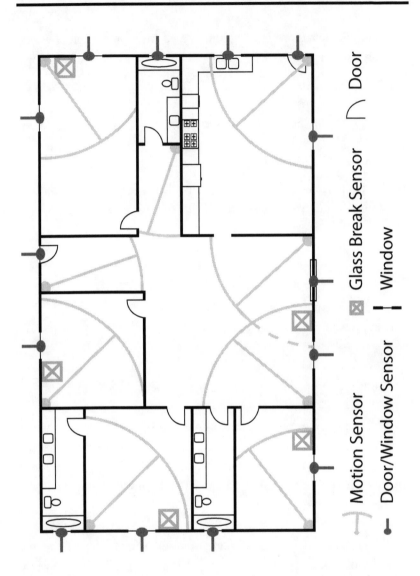

Figure 2 - Sample Sensor Layout

Phone Protocols

Just as with the exterior of your home, do no broadcast your name in the phonebook or online. Pay the extra dollar to have an unlisted phone number. This keeps your name as well as your contact information out of many publications. Retain as much control over who knows where you live and your numbers. A significant problem is that phone books are no longer restricted to the region in which you live. Phone information services make every phone number national and every phone listing is available on the Internet, making it international. Once on the Internet, always on the Internet. There is no going back. Do not leave a trail and do not make it easy for stalkers.

Similarly, do not give away information on your answering machine. You have no idea who is calling or what he or she wants, so refrain from giving away personal information to complete strangers. For example, do not leave a message with something along the lines of, "You've reached Jack and Mary's house," or worse, "Missy, Bethy and Amanda aren't in right now." The rule also applies to children. DO NOT let children record answering machine messages. It may sound cute, but such a message empowers criminals with your personal details. Do not provide stalkers, criminals, scam artists, kidnappers and pedophiles with information that can be used against you. Information on your answering machine may as well be posted on a billboard in your front yard. If a criminal wants information about you, make him work for it. Be more trouble than you are worth. Be a hard target.

Women living alone, single mothers, and groups of women sharing an apartment should have a brother, father, or boyfriend record the answering machine message. A public recording should be an adult male voice and provide no details. Provide nothing more than the phone number, which they should already have since the caller dialed it. For example, my home message only states "You have reached 555-123-4567. Please leave a message." It meets the need of a message without providing any details as to where you are or what you might be doing. The person on the other end has no idea and the goal is to keep it that way.

Do not ever say you are gone on vacation or out of town for the holidays. The last thing we want to do is alert any criminal that the home is vacant for any period of time, even if it is for 10 minutes.

Remember that no one is required to answer the phone in our personal lives. It is OK to let the phone ring and go to voice-mail. People have been ingrained with an overriding urge to drop what they are doing to pick up the handset when that ringer goes off. Fight that urge. Nothing horrible is going to happen if you let it ring. A call can always be returned.

If you have children do not let them answer the phone. Children are naïve and can be manipulated into providing personal information including addresses, where they go to school, their names, how old they are, where their parents work, phone numbers and everything else stored in their sponge-like brains. It only takes a few lies and all will be laid bare. Please, DO NOT let children answer the phone.

The next protocol is that the man of the house is always home, he is just indisposed, cannot make it to the phone at the moment, or will call the person back later. If you are a woman alone or with children you never want to broadcast that your boyfriend, husband or father is out of the house. They are always home and just cannot get to the phone just then. Do not say why and do not make up excuses; just keep it simple and say generically he cannot speak right now. He could be napping, working in the yard or in the shower, but you do not have to provide a reason. You are in control of the information and if you start making something up it will sound questionable. Most people, especially friends or business associates, will accept a simple statement and the conversation will end.

If the caller pushes for a time for a return call just say you cannot be certain, but will deliver the message. If the caller becomes really pushy, your intuition alarms should be going off. Why is the caller pushing you so hard for a time? What do you know about this caller? Remember that he or she called you, you are the one in the position of power, so do not let a voice on the other end of the phone intimidate or pressure you. Be firm, be confident and end the conversation, or just hang up.

It is acceptable to be rude. This goes against our mother's conditioning to always be nice, but criminals will use social conditioning to manipulate well-adjusted, normal citizens. The best defense against this type of manipulation is to be rude. It is perfectly acceptable to not answer the phone and it is perfectly acceptable to hang up on people who you do not know or are trying to manipulate you.

For example, if you answer and the person who called you asks something like, "Is the Man or Woman of the house home?" Hang-up. If the caller does not know whom he or she is calling, then that caller is fishing for information and speaking with him or her is not advisable. The one question that really gets me is when I answer and the first thing the caller asks is, "Who is this?" I have three responses to that question:

1) Hang-up.
2) You tell me, you called here.
3) Well who the <expletive> are you?

Remember that you have no proof that the person on the other end of the phone is who he or she claims to be. None. They are just a voice from the ether. Caller ID numbers and names can be spoofed with $10 technologies. Caller ID is not a reliable source of information or any sort of proof of identity.

One of the ways charities make money is by selling their lists of donators to other charities. It is just part of the system. As a result, unknown charities can call looking for a donation that can be put right onto a credit card over the phone. Chances are this person who has a name and knows that money has been given to them in the past is legitimate. However, provide a credit card number only when *you* contact *them*. Initiate the interaction. The caller could be anyone from anywhere in the world and there is no way of verifying his or her identity. If you have an interest in helping them out, request the organization send an invoice. This is also a good way to verify they have your address. Not having your home address is a scam indicator. Then, in a week or so a nice letter will arrive in the mail from the charity reporting a pledge and requesting a check. The charity gets their donation and I have kept my credit card number from being stolen.

Emergency Services

Your mobile phone is a lifeline and your #1 defensive weapon, so keep it close and keep it available to you. Should the need to call emergency services for help arise, you must provide them with specific and life-saving information:

1) Where you are with enough detail to find you.

This is the first and most important piece of information you can provide. First, although calling the service is supposed to bring up your address, that part of the system may be offline for some reason, or it may not be available in your area (which is rare in the US these days, but it does happen). Therefore, do not assume Emergency Services knows your location so tell them. Another consideration is that the information in the system may be wrong. It is rare, but it has happened. In one instance a fire truck went to the wrong home because they received bad directions from the system and they spent 20 minutes looking for the home while it burned.

Also consider you might be calling from your cell phone. You could be anywhere in the world with a cell phone. In theory, you could speak with a 911-operator in Miami, but be in Mexico.

In an example closer to home, what could happen when calling from a hotel room. Certainly, the hotel's address will come up on their system, but not necessarily the room number. If you are in a Las Vegas-style hotel there could be hundreds of rooms. One might face the same scenario in an office building. The building address will come up, but which floor, which office or which cubical?

2) Tell the operator the situation.
It is a heart attack, a home invader or an injury? Is the burglary *in progress*? Report in progress. If you do not tell the operator the robbery is in progress, he or she might assume it happened earlier and you are reporting it after the fact. You will get faster attention if Emergency Services understands the *intruder is still in the home and the **event is in progress**.*

CASE STUDY

An individual reported a burglary and it was 3 days before the local police station sent someone to take a report (it was a civilian, not even a uniformed police officer).

3) Your name.
Let Emergency Services know who you are. Among other things, this helps establish you as the victim.

4) If you are a woman alone, report it.
A woman alone in distress is a high priority call and will be treated with the upmost priority.

Security experts recommend writing out a script and keeping it by the bedside phone or inside the safe room. The concept is that you might be too stressed to think clearly and cover all of the details, but you can just read a script that contains all of the information without having to think too much.

Do not lie or exaggerate calls into Emergency Services to get them to show up faster. It is true that someone walking through your backyard or loitering on your front lawn will not get as fast a response as someone breaking into your home. However, do not lie to Emergency Services and tell them the guy is breaking in when he is not. Lying to Emergency Services in some circumstances may be illegal and can result in fines.

Dogs

I love dogs. I grew up with dogs. Dogs are great deterrents for most criminals and wonderful biological alarms. However, dogs are living, breathing creatures and as such have their own personalities and are fallible. Not all dogs are cut out for security duty. It is a reflection of personality and temperament. Every breed is different and every individual is different.

The other problem is most dogs are cowards. They may put on a good show, but ask any law enforcement or security officer who has had to hop a fence in pursuit of a criminal or investigate suspicious behavior and we learn that a confident presence, a sharp word and a threatening motion will get most dogs to back off. The dogs may not stop barking and growling at you, but it will be from a distance. Many dogs can be driven off with a splash of pepper spray or a whack on the nose with a heavy flashlight. Occasionally there is the real protector and none of that will dissuade it. That is probably less than 10% of the population.

As recounted in the Preface, when my home was burglarized and burned to the ground, the criminals drugged our two dogs. They could just have well been shot or otherwise killed. Our dogs offered a level of protection, but not complete unto itself and that is a mistake that many people make. Many people think, "I have a big dog, I don't need a gun, lights or an alarm system." This is not the case. We should never place too much emphasis on a single security measure. Dogs are but one piece of the solution set, not a solutions unto themselves.

CASE STUDY

My parents have a wonderful dog, a Dalmatian, who is the best dog with kids I have ever seen. She is wonderfully gentle and incredibly patient. She is also hard of hearing and completely useless as a guard dog. My parent's cats are better at alerting them to when someone has arrived than the dog. The cats will perk their ears up and meow minutes before the dog reacts. I can walk into the home and the cats will greet me at the door, but I can walk down the hallway and into my parent's bedroom before the dog will raise her head and bark a greeting. She is a great family member, but completely useless for protection.

CASE STUDY

My sister keeps several dogs for home protection and hunting. She trains them and even wins obedience competitions with them. One, a Black Labrador, will make more noise than a police siren and act ferocious if a stranger approaches. The problem is the dog will be putting on the show from three feet behind you.

She also has a huge, sweet Doberman. This dog will let anyone onto her property. It could be the mailman, gardener, meter readers or whomever. However, anyone reaching for a doorknob will be greeted with a gut-wrenching growl. If the "visitor" then makes the mistake of trying to open the door, he or she will lose a limb.

CASE STUDY

A family was vacationing at Lake Tahoe. The brother brought one of his dogs: a big, friendly, yellow Labrador. A friend of the family was going to join them for a few days. As he was going to arrive late while the family was out to dinner, a key was stashed so that he could wait inside until the family returned. The dog was in the house, but no one considered it a problem as the dog had met this friend before and the home was different. Why would a dog defend someplace that was not his home from someone he had met before? This was a critical error in judgment.

The friend was in his 60s. When he entered the rental house, the 110-pound Labrador attacked him. Fortunately, this man was not your average 60-year old. He was career military and a combat veteran of two wars, serving on the ground in the Army Infantry. He received three Purple Hearts during multiple combat tours. He retired as a full Colonel in the Army Military Police. When he wore his Dress Blues, the only decoration he wore was his Combat Infantry Badge. Although technically not out of uniform, no other award mattered, not even his purple hearts.

The good news is the dog did not hurt him. He was pretty spry, dodged the initial attack and escaped outside. It then became a game for the friend. While it may have been a game for him, it was not for the dog. The big dog wanted to rip his throat out. Using diversionary tactics, he managed to trick the dog into a room and lock him in it. When the family returned, he was relaxing on the couch, beer in hand with a snarling monster throwing a fit in the next room. The dog would not accept him and the two had to remain separated for the remainder of the vacation.

When the friend visited two months later, the dog still remembered him and even lunged at him. After some work and more time, the dog eventually accepted him.

The point of the story is to illustrate that even if the dog is hell-bent on protecting the home, they can be outsmarted. In the case of my home burglary, they can also be drugged.

If you do not own a dog, you can leverage dogs in your neighborhood, especially if you have one living next door. If a normally quiet dog starts barking at an odd time or in the middle of the night, pay attention. Something out of the ordinary is happening. Do not discount a barking dog simply because it does not belong to you. The dog could be barking at an intruder who just jumped your wall.

In the earlier mentioned sexual assault case the lady thought she heard her neighbor's dog barking. It was a passing comment during the interview, but important enough that she remembered it and mentioned it months later.

Safe Rooms

Anyone breaking into your home may be carrying a weapon. It could be a lead pipe, a knife, or even a gun. The person is breaking the law and he is entering into a potentially dangerous and conflict situation, he may bring protection for himself. He may not use it, he may not even want to use it, but there is a chance he has something for himself and could care less about how you fare at the end of the exchange. Do not think for an instant that someone who has the gall to enter your home is some fashionable "cat burglar." Most likely the goon is there to take what they can sell quickly and that he is already intoxicated either with drugs or alcohol or both. Or worse yet, that they are there to hurt you in addition to taking your belongings.

Once this person is in your home, what should you do? First, call 911 for help. The next step should be to hole up, hunker down and wait for them to arrive. Of course, if the individual comes after you, you are within your rights to defend yourself and your family.

Home invasions are dangerous and fluid situations. There is no right, wrong or perfect answer. Every home has a unique floor plan and every situation is different, so you must use your own good judgment to protect yourself and your family members.

One protective measure is to build a safe room in your home. It needs to be a safe haven, but not necessarily a $50,000 bunker. In most cases what is required is a designated room that everyone in the household knows is the meeting place. It needs to be defensible. In many cases all that is required is to replace the normal inside, flimsy, hollow doors with a solid-core exterior door and install a good deadbolt. Replacing the wood doorframe with a steel frame so that it cannot be kicked in is another option.

In many circumstances the master bedroom is considered the Safe Room. However, young children cannot be expected to navigate a home in a crisis situation. The risk of a child bumping into an intoxicated criminal in a dark hallway when the home's alarm triggers is too great. Therefore, the parents must go to the child or children. Once the children are collected, it is unsafe to navigate back across the home to the master bedroom. Therefore, it might be best to establish the child's bedroom as the Safe Room.

Another defensive tactic to consider is stashing weapons throughout the home. The concept is that you never know where you will be when an incident occurs. Should something happen, defensive tools are required immediately and seconds can matter. A trusty baseball bat at the bedside when sleeping may be on the other side of the house and up a staircase if you are up late watching TV in the living room when the window breaks.

Do not stash weapons around the home or even in the safe room without first considering child access. Kids and weapons do not mix. The last thing we want to have happen is for a child to pick up a firearm or knife and play with it. Any defensive weapon should be quickly available, but also secured against child access. That is a pretty tall order and may be impossible in your home. Stashing weapons throughout the home may not be a viable option for homes with children. Use your own judgment and keep your children safe.

Understand that it can take a long time for law enforcement to show up. Even once they are on site, it can take even longer before they will enter the home. Reality is very different from a 2-minute response time with officers kicking in the front door to hunt down the criminal and save the damsel in distress that we see on TV or in the movies. Officers are human and want to return to their families with all of their parts at the end of their shifts. They will often take their time to ensure as much safety as possible for the officers before entering the home. This means an even longer wait for you and to some extent a risk of being accidentally shot by the responding officers.

CASE STUDY

For example, it took law enforcement 45-minutes to respond to a 911-call that a man had broken into a lone woman's home.

She was home alone and walked into her kitchen to find a man standing there, naked, spattered with mud and completely incoherent. She ran, holed up in her master bedroom, and called 911. After the 45-minute wait for the police to arrive, it was another 20 minutes before they cleared her home. She had to hide in her bedroom for over an hour before she could move.

Door Protocols

When someone knocks at the door, the first guideline is to never open the door until the identity of the person(s) on the other side have been established and he, she or they have been identified as a non-threat. So how do we do that?

First, use remote viewing devices such as video cameras, peepholes and windows. Once you have seen the person, back away from the door. Distance is your friend in a conflict situation so do not stay right up against the door. If the person on the other side kicks in or shoots through the door, the closer you are the more likely you are to be hit. Back away 5 to 10 feet away from the door. Furthermore, step off to the side so that you are not directly in line with the door. Again, this is to create distance and an angle so that if something comes through the door you are less likely to get hit.

Next, challenge the person through the door (at this point the door is still shut). A gruff, "who is it?" is enough. Let the "visitor" know your home is occupied by a jerk or bitch and that you are more trouble than expected. This will help encourage them to move on. Additionally, listen not to just what they say, but how they say it. Tone can be an indicator of intent. If you do not like what you hear, send them away and you have never exposed yourself directly to the unknown. Plus, the person on the other side of the door has not seen into the home.

Children should *never* answer the door and it is best if they remain out of sight if the door is opened to an unknown entity.

CASE STUDY

A person was home alone one afternoon and received a heavy knock on the door. As he passed a window on the way to the door he noticed a large man standing away from the door in the driveway. This set his intuition to screaming. Without getting too close to the door the homeowner called out, "Who is it?" and the response was, "Delivery."

Something was wrong. Everything was off. Why were there two of them? The knock was heavy and aggressive. Furthermore, UPS, Fed-X and the Postal Service always identify themselves. They say, "UPS," "Fed-X" or "Mailman" or "Postal Service," never, "Delivery."

Then the homeowner noticed the 3rd large man and several red flags were apparent.

The homeowner called out, "Who is it for?" The guy responded with some name that he had never heard before and said he did not know him and that the person did not live there.

The knocker grew angry and his tone was hostile. "Do you know where he is?" The man outside pressed further by claiming he was an "officer of the court" and he wanted to know where he could find this guy.

Again, the response was no.

He then gave up and walked away. He was heard telling the other men in the driveway that the address they had was several years old and that the homeowner did not know where their prey was living.

These guys were probably bounty hunters and after someone who had lived at that address years before, or they just had bad information. Bounty hunters work within the legal system, but can be heavy handed at times and are not bound by many of the restrictions placed upon sworn law enforcement. They live and work within the grey area of the justice system so keeping them on the other side of the door was appropriate.

A complete conversation can be carried out and come to a resolution without exposing yourself directly to some stranger knocking on the door. If you do not have to open your door, do not. It is far safer to leave it closed.

Criminals have been known to lie (I know it sounds far fetched, but it happens). If someone comes to your door and claims to have been attacked, their car is broken down or they are lost do not open the door. Just tell them that you will call 911 and get help for them. Listen to their response. Do they respond with, "Great. Thank you!" or "I do not need them, but thanks anyway." With either response, you might want to call 911 anyway. Either this person needs help which is best provided by a trained professional, or he/she is running some sort of scam and the police might want to check them out. You must decide what to do. However, do not open the door and expose yourself to a potential threat.

Strangers as Guests

Inviting strangers into your home is always risky. Strangers are delivery people, salesmen, repairmen, gardener or charities. It is an odd thing, but people often do not look at service or repair people as being "strangers" or potential threats. Take a moment to think about this person invited into the home. In reality, you know nothing about them. You might not even know the company he or she works for.

One might believe that company loyalty might prevent such occurrences. They would not hire a known criminal. Often large corporations will do background checks on employees hired to prevent potential liability issues in negligent hiring practices. Generally, large corporations are intent on hiring honest individuals and will perform good background checks. If they subcontract delivery services or home installations, they should ensure that the subcontracting company is licensed and bonded. As a homeowner it is always advisable to ensure any company hired to do any home repair is both licensed and bonded.

The challenge is that employee background checks are done at the time of hiring and rarely repeated throughout employment. Things can change in a person's life in just a few years. The employee with a spotless record might have become addicted to drugs, fallen-in with the wrong crowd, accrued massive amounts of debt or even become indebted to the wrong people since the background check performed years ago. In realty, you do not know this person and the employer probably does not either.

CASE STUDY

A young man was moving from his mother's home and packing, including a semi-automatic rifle. The rifle was laying out on his bed and full view when some workmen his mother had invited in walked by his open door. These workmen were there to pick up some old furniture for a national charity and were employed by this charity. As the workmen passed by, they stopped and stared at the rifle, whistled and made some other comments, then went about their business collecting the furniture and left.

The very next day, "someone" broke the home and ransacked the young man's room. They tore the place up. They did not venture into any other part of the home. Fortunately, they left empty-handed the individual had already moved the guns to his new home. The young man is convinced, based upon the actions of the workmen, that they were the ones who broke into the home. He even told the police that when they showed up (because a gun was involved, an actual policeman took the report), but they did nothing other than take a report as there was no theft. In the end, the crime was just breaking and entering with no loss of property.

Donate clothes and furniture to charities, but deliver it to one of their drop-off stations, or if it is too large, move it outside of the home to the driveway and do not invite them in. Same end result, but a little safer.

If workmen do not need to come inside the home, do not let them.

If workmen have been in the home, check to ensure that doors and windows are shut and locked appropriately. Criminals invited into the home for legitimate work will often unlock windows during their activities to make it easier to enter the home later. They might also take house keys and garage door openers if exposed (opportunistic).

CASE STUDY

A homeowner discovered an unlocked window after carpet cleaners left the home. It was a window on the front of the house that was never used. The window was closed, the blinds we pulled, but the latch was left unlocked. Another homeowner had a window in their garage left open after plumbers worked on the water heater. Alarm systems can alert when doors and windows are left open, but not unlocked. Check all doors and windows after workmen have left the premises.

CASE STUDY

A quick search of the Internet reveals hundreds of cases where workmen invited into the home have assaulted women. In 1999 there was a case where an employee of a huge international retail corporation raped the woman homeowner instead of cleaning her carpets.

When workmen are in the home, use the following precautions:

* Do not let them wander throughout the house
* Close the doors to rooms they do not need to be in
* Do not leave valuables lying around
* Remove purses or wallets from sight

If you feel uncomfortable, trust your instinct. Say something has come up and he needs to leave. Now. Remember that it is OK to be rude if necessary.

The chances of being assaulted or robbed by a professional installer are slim. They are even slimmer if the workman is licensed and bonded. However, everyone should be aware of these types of crimes so that we can take preventative measures to protect themselves. One cannot live in fear of everything, but take steps to protect oneself. Ignorance is no shield, but we can implement a few safety precautions that are.

Be aware that the attack may not happen at the initial contact.

CASE STUDY

A woman was raped in her home by a handyman she had hired many times to do repair work in her home. He crawled in through her doggy door during the day, ransacked the home and then repeatedly attacked her over several hours when she returned from work. This was someone she had employed several times and had gained her trust.

Inside Lights

Lights inside the home are visible from the outside, even with window coverings. They make the home look occupied and active. Many people set their lights on timers when they leave on vacation to make it look like they are still home. This can be good as well as bad.

A predictable schedule is bad (as mentioned in a previous section). When going to bed and turning off the light at the exact time every night, a stalker or home invader can figure this out. If leaving the home at the same time every morning or taking the exactly same route home at the exact the same time every day, can be tracked. Lights on timers do the same thing, but you can turn some of that to your advantage.

The technique is to run lights on timers all the time, not just when leaving town. That way, there is home activity when the lights turn off and on automatically. It will be harder for anyone looking to determine if one is gone for the weekend, out at a late dinner, sitting at home reading or on a holiday.

Another technique is to set the timers at odd intervals. Humans are regimented and habitual. We tend to think in nice round numbers. We learn to set a light timer to trigger at round numbers: on the hour, half-hour or 15-minute increments. However, actions can be more random than that. While a nightly news program may end at 9:30pm, we do not get up from the couch and hit the light switch the moment the program ends. So why set the timer like that? The timer should simulate natural actions as much as possible, so set timers at odd numbers, such as 9:36pm.

When retiring for the night, notice how much time it takes to move from room to room and turn the lights off. Then set timers to mimic those time differentials. All the lights in the house turning off at exactly 9:30pm is suspicious. But lights in rooms turning off in a somewhat irregular sequence looks more like someone is walking down the hall turning them off by hand.

Some timer systems have a random element built in to simulate our normal, random actions. The timer is set for 9:45pm it will trigger randomly within 10 minutes before or after the defined time. Be certain to check the label of any light timer purchased to determine the random interval, or if it has a random interval setting.

Light emitted by televisions can be seen through window coverings. There are devices on the market now that simulate television lights. The more advanced models simulate the moving action of the screen. The current market leader is FakeTV (www.faketv.com). For $30, a small box will simulate the activity and motion of a large television using power-efficient LEDs. The unit also has a light sensor so that it can be set to turn on automatically when a room goes dark and turn off when room is lit by a lamp or natural light.

Television simulators are a fantastic an inexpensive way of making the home look active and occupied. They require far less power than an active television, are small (a mere 4-inch cube) and can be set to turn themselves on and off.

Creating an Inventory

Having an inventory of items in the home is important and could be critical in obtaining the appropriate amount of replacement money from your insurance company. Creating a home inventory does not need require an immense amount of effort, paperwork, or logging.

The easiest way create a detailed inventory is with a home video camera. Put in a fresh tape, walk the home and just talk about each item. Whenever possible, zoom in on the make, model and serial number. If the serial number is too small to show in the screen, read it aloud. Insurance companies love video tape inventories because they can see the item, see its condition and it is harder to fake video than photographs. When done, just make a few copies of the tape and *store it away from the home*. Keep one master copy in a safe, but store at least one copy off premises in a safe deposit box. In the event of a natural disaster, the bank vaults are so well constructed, they can survive most anything Mother Nature delivers.

The video inventory can generally be completed in 90 minutes or less and well worth the time. Record anything of value from computers, televisions, the video camera itself, furniture, jewelry; anything you can be compensated for from your insurance policy.

Law enforcement also recommends engraving your driver's license number on anything that might be taken for quick cash. It will just make it that much harder for the criminal to fence if it is marked. Police do check pawnshops for stolen merchandise. Also, please *do not mark items with your social security number*, just your driver's license number. If your state uses the Social Security Number as the driver's license number, ask for an alternative.

If stolen, there is a slim chance that your items will be recovered. It does happen, cars have a fairly high recovery rate, but small items tend to just disappear.

Professional criminals will sometimes return to burglarize homes a second time. The property has been marked as a "soft target" containing valuables. The will wait a few months until the insurance money has been paid and the stolen items have been replaced, then hit the home a second time, repeating the process they used the first time. It is critical to increase the security around the home after any burglary. Make it apparent that the home has become a "hard target" and that it is not worth the effort to strike a second time.

Distraction Robberies

There is a surprising type of common home invasion that few people think about. It is not the normal kick in the front door, smash a window or pick a lock type of burglary. In these cases the victims openly invite the criminals into their homes. This type of crime is universal across all cities and countries. I have received emails from listeners of my weekly podcast, Practical Defense, from all over the world relating this method of criminals receiving invitations into the home in order to remove property. How does it work? Social Engineering.

A typical scenario is one in which the criminal assumes the role of an authority figure. The authority figure is nothing too overpowering such as law enforcement or fire department as that would raise concern. Usually the criminals pose as a representative from the power, water, electric, phone, natural gas or cable TV company. Other times, they pose as collector for charity or someone looking to provide services such as gardening or tree trimming.

The goal is to get you to open your door and invite the criminal inside, or get you to walk outside, leaving your door open. This works because of social engineering. We are taught from a young age to respect those in authority, to obey their commands without question, to be nice and to help others. It is how our society works and the reason we can have 20 million people living in close proximity without everyone snapping. Criminals are aware of this conditioning and use it. Therefore, when a person from an "official" city utility shows up on our doorstep unannounced and requests to come inside to check the water, electricity or natural gas because of a reported problem in the neighborhood, we invite them right in and offer them a glass of lemonade. We do not ask to see a work order or check identification because that would be rude. We comply with the requests and literally invite the wolf into the henhouse.

There are numerous police reports of these types of crimes. The process follows a fairly consistent pattern. It is during the day and the target is usually, but not always, a retired elderly person. The team of criminals knocks on the door, expecting someone to be home. When the victim answers the door, the criminal explains that there is a problem with some utility in the neighborhood and they are paying a courtesy call to check how the victim is doing and if the services are working. The criminal then asks to come inside to check the service. The victim is more than happy to let pleasant "city worker" in the house.

Once inside, the primary criminal takes the victim to a distant room to check the service. It could be as simple as a back bathroom to check to see if the water is running, checking the light switch in a bedroom or the gas in kitchen. Once the victim is distracted and in another room, the partner quickly steals whatever he can grab. This includes wallets, jewelry, cash, watches and anything small with value. Other items taken are keys and garage door openers for potential future thefts. After a few minutes, the criminals leave and the victim eventually notices the crime.

We may scoff at the idea of this happening, but this crime happens daily in major cities all over the world. Social engineering is a powerful tool and even the most intelligent can be caught off guard.

Things you can do identify this type of criminal activity:

• Look for a service truck parked in front of the home
  Companies want advertising and city vehicles are always clearly marked. If you do not see a truck that should be associated with the person at your door, do not let them in.

- Ask for a business card
- Ask for identification
  Find out who this person is. A criminal will not want to be identified. An employee will not mind.
- Ask for paperwork
  Service people always have paperwork (printed or electronic). Ask to see the work order.
- Challenge them in some way
  Criminals are looking for an easy score. As soon as you appear to be a hard target, they will likely move on to an easier victim.

Apartments

In the United States, you *are not required* to let this person into your home. Only the police with a lawful search warrant issued by a judge or probable cause can enter your home without your permission. Even if you rent, the homeowners must give you 24-hours notice before they can enter the home. You even have to sign a release to let them enter your property without notice in the event of an emergency.

Service companies have the right to access their meters, but those are always on the outside of the building for a reason; they are never on the inside. The cable and satellite TV companies do not have the right to come into your home to check the boxes sitting next to your television. Entry into your home is by invitation only.

One can be polite, courteous and comply with a request, just be aware and verify.

The term "apartment" can mean different things to different people so here are some other terms to describe multi-family living complexes: Condominium, apartment (rental or own), duplex, townhouse, flat, dormitory, hotel, etc. In this section the term apartment will be used for any shared living space in a common building.

Apartment buildings, especially "nice" buildings with obvious security measures can give a false sense of security. The greatest security risk with these shared spaces is that security becomes a shared responsibility. Other residents can leave perimeter doors open which puts everyone in the building at risk. One opened door or gate can give a criminal the opportunity to hurt others, emotionally or physically.

In both rental apartments and owned condominiums and I have found that owners are more aware of security than renters. When owning something, a person is more likely to treat it better than someone renting.

The conservative approach is to assume that strangers walk the common halls. Look to personal space and secure it as best as possible regardless of the security provided by the building management or homeowners association. Review all entry points to the dwelling including windows and not just to doors. For example, do the balconies connect? If not, is the space between them close enough for a person to jump across?

If a door is not secure enough or the lock is faulty, submit a complaint in writing. Putting a complaint in writing makes it formal and traceable. Be certain to include words and phrases such as, "safety risk" or "security risk." Those types of words are more likely to get the attention of management and attorneys. If a specific risk is identified in writing and management did nothing to address it in a timely manner and something happens to you, it could lead to a negligence complaint. Always keep a hard (print) copy of the letter for yourself.

When writing do not make the letter aggressive or threatening; be polite, specific and factual. Include photos if you can. Simply state that you would like to bring the following items to their attention, they place residents at risk and request that the issue be addressed in a timely fashion. Leave it at that and see what the response is and escalate from there if necessary through an association or management company.

Request the locks be re-keyed when you move in. Keys stamped, "Do not duplicate," are a joke and cannot be trusted. If management says it is too expensive, offer to cover the cost. Again, put it in writing. Never forget that you have no idea who occupied that space before you.

Non-invasive alarm systems can be installed. There are many high-quality alarm systems that are self-install and 100% wireless. Even the connection to the monitoring center is via digital cellular and you can take the system with you when you move.

There are several factors to consider when selecting an apartment or even single-family home. First, avoid buildings near freeways and highways. The reason for this is that freeways are escape routes for criminals. After committing a crime, the criminal wants to put as much space between them and the crime scene and the fastest route is the freeway or highway. One of the police responses to a robbery is to hit the nearest freeway and check every speeder to see if the vehicle matches the description of the criminal's getaway car.

Avoid high traffic areas that may attract petty robbery and theft activity. For example, avoid areas such as gas stations, convenience stores, liquor stores, bars and fast food restaurants. Try to select a building at least four blocks from any of those establishments; the greater the distance, the greater the general security. Additionally, look for buildings a few blocks in from any main boulevard. According to crime reports, burglaries and thefts drop off significantly 3 or more blocks in from a major street. They are not non-existent, but they are less.

Avoid buildings near high schools. Teenagers believe they are incapable of being hurt or caught and petty crime tends to be higher in areas immediately around high schools. Petty thefts, car break-ins (stolen stereos, smash and grabs) are more common around high schools than areas one-mile from the school.

Also, in larger cities there is often a gang element that can develop in the high schools. One school district implemented a plan a few decades ago to diversify the city. The goal was to mix the population of the districts to expand awareness and build community. Kids from underprivileged neighborhoods were bussed to schools in high-income neighborhoods to expose them to better living conditions and vice versa. One of the unintended consequences of this system was that it spread gangs across the city and sometimes put rival gangs in the same school.

Therefore, an excellent location for an apartment, from a security perspective, would be away from freeway onramps, convenience stores, fast food restaurants, gas stations and high schools, and three or more blocks in from any major street. In many areas, that is a high standard to meet and often (and unfortunately) impossible to find. There is no perfect location; only the best selection from what is available.

Here are a few quick items look for inside the building when visiting before a final decision. This only takes only a minute or so when inspecting the building:

- How does the intercom work?
  Is it a separate system or does it tie into the phone system? If it ties into the phone system, be careful what you say on your telephone answering machine. A recorded message saying, "Hi, we're not home right now," to someone on the doorstep is not a good idea.
- Are any doors propped open that should be closed?

- How clean is it?
  This speaks to maintenance and attention to detail.
- Does it have video surveillance?
  Ask if the cameras are recording and where the tapes are kept.
- Is the garage secured?
- Where are the elevators and stairwells in relation to the apartment?
  Stairways are the freeway onramps of buildings.
- Do the apartments have individual security systems installed?
  This is rare, but really nice when found.

PRIORITIES

Home burglaries and robberies are traumatic. It can take years to fully recover from an event. The burglary and burning of a home at age ten has had a lifelong impact upon a family. Today they are still highly sensitive to the smell of smoke in the home and drop everything until they can identify the source. It is a heightened sense of security. Experiences have ingrained a healthy awareness of the criminal element and how truly vulnerable individuals are.

Take precautions, install alarms, train dogs, build walls and safe rooms, but the best plans can and do fail. Remember that the primary reason for erecting those barriers is to keep the bad people from our families, not our objects. Walk away from everything owned without hesitation if it means keeping the family safe. One can start over from nothing. It takes time, but it can be done.

Losing a ring to a criminal is painful. Losing a child or loved-one because a person is too pig-headed to give up a ring is a pain that will never go away. Keep your family at the top of your home security priority list. Things can be replaced, people cannot.

RECOMMENDED READING

Ayoob, M. (1980). *In the Gravest Extreme: The Role of the Firearm in Personal Protection.* Concord, NH: Police Bookshelf.

Ayoob, M. (1983). *The Truth About Self Protection.* Concord, NH: Police Bookshelf.

de Becker, G. (1997). *The Gift of Fear and Other Survival Signals that Protect Us From Violence.* Boston, MA: Little, Brown and Company.

Greene, J. (2010). *DEFY the Bad Guy Powerful Practical Self-Defense Strategies for Every Woman.* Fairfax, VA: Julie Greene Personal Safety Solutions.

Grossman, D. (1995) *On Killing: The Psychological Cost of Learning to Kill in War and Society.* Boston, MA: Little, Brown and Company.

Wagner, J. (2005). *Reality-Based Personal Protection.* Los Angeles, CA: Black Belt Books.

Wong, D. (2006). *Knife Laws of the Fifty States: A Guide for the Law-Abiding Traveler.* Bloomington, IN: AuthorHouse.

OTHER WORKS BY ALEX HADDOX

Practical Defense

A free weekly podcast (Internet radio show). Practical Defense is a podcast that provides a practical approach to staying safe in our increasingly dangerous urban environments. Learn simple strategies and everyday habits from Alex Haddox that will help protect you and your loved ones from harm. Hear interviews with experts on the criminal mind and listen to stories directly from real victims. When you understand what a criminal looks for in a target, you can avoid taking on those characteristics and thus escape selection. Available for free in iTunes, Zune Marketplace and from the web: http://www.alexhaddox.com/podcast

Raising Awareness

A recurring column in Tae Kwon Do Times magazine on the subjects of awareness, avoidance and self-protection techniques to stay safe. http://www.taekwondotimes.com

Made in the USA
Charleston, SC
20 December 2011